Green is the Orator

The publisher gratefully acknowledges the generous support of the College of Arts and Sciences at Case Western Reserve University.

SARAH GRIDLEY

Green is the Orator

 University of California Press   Berkeley   Los Angeles   London

University of California Press, one of the most distinguished university presses in the United States, enriches lives around the world by advancing scholarship in the humanities, social sciences, and natural sciences. Its activities are supported by the UC Press Foundation and by philanthropic contributions from individuals and institutions. For more information, visit www.ucpress.edu.

University of California Press
Berkeley and Los Angeles, California

University of California Press, Ltd.
London, England

For acknowledgments of previous publication, please see page 89.

Library of Congress Cataloging-in-Publication Data

Gridley, Sarah, 1968–.
    Green is the orator / Sarah Gridley.
        p.   cm. — (New California poetry ; 29)
    ISBN 978-0-520-26241-6 (cloth : alk. paper)
    ISBN 978-0-520-26242-3 (pbk. : alk. paper)
    1. Nature—Poetry.   I. Title.

PS3607.R525G74   2010
811'.6—dc22   2009037667

Manufactured in the United States of America

19   18
10   9   8   7   6   5   4   3   2

The paper used in this publication meets the minimum requirements of ANSI/NISO Z39.48–1992 (R 1997) (*Permanence of Paper*).

For life- and love-giving mothers, in the biologic and cosmic realizations of the word. For Beecher, Elizabeth, Julie, Kitsey, Laure, Linda, Martha, Patricia, and Mom.

Contents

ONE

He is hell become heaven, becoming hell; he is evolution, a matter of energy, a star in the dark tomb, a shadow cast by sunlight. He is life that cannot be contained, a holy insurrection, blessed negativity.

Coefficient

About the star-cold abundance of August sand—

this spell of my two hands working in the dark
I liken to the feeling of your two hands working
behind me, or your two hands coming before me
in the white mirth of bright drapes, white lengths
the wind sends in salt-light through the feeling
your two hands have in coming to find me.

There are things I liken to crossbeams

inside of things I call politeness, things I liken to super-
intendence, seashells, pale hosts of erosions, fadings
I liken to insight. There in the window
of your soloist house, I think that nothing
is holding up

this thought that is feeling you moving.

Salt Marsh, Thick with Behaviors

In seasoned assertion, the red-winged calling of the grass.
From spaces outside the territory, the stone summons,

the stone sum. Weight is a quality known to boundary's
swerve. The sum of which is fragile: waves leave mica

stuck to skin. Some I know of inherence. Some
I have not remembered. Among the lightest of insects,

a Comma has a cryptic edge. *A woman should behave herself,*
naturally. In mica, the glamorous stammer of mirror—

A woman should behave herself naturally. Bill-tilt,
check-call, songspread—a bone flute snapped

from passage of bird—the unearthed
played unearthly.

Table of Consanguinity (The Cousin Chart)

Once they are there,
the bearings are theirs, the sickness peculiar to motion
removed by horizon's evident flatness.

What they bear is the date, and whatever will follow.
Bay of gray margins, mobile as curfew. Rollick of tides
and empty casements. Stone-deaf stones marking thoughts

out loud. Schist like a book of tempers.
Stars in dogged pantomime.
Exactly what

the waves were for lengthening.
Slow, elemental line. Gray like the saint of a put-out fire.
Sea of gray margins, solemn as seals. On it a flash

like something wrong. On it the falling quiet.
What they touch is the moss
like an earthly expense.

Green in a poise
almost vernacular, almost the sensible
guide to North.

Diminution of the Clear Thing

My somnolence is
the rest of trees (sessile touch around dry leaf
    to know my weirdest passiveness). To go the irises
      the pebbled drive the luminous

claps into valley.
When you have posted a letter in the open air,
    an artist will know your feeling,
      will ground the clouds in canines of noon,

gold leaf pressured over graphite sun.
To feel outside an envelope—
    unchangeable corner mailbox blue—
      there are words in the morning against

the mind, containing sleep
in the shape of walking. A nomenclature castle opens to sky:
    grassy crenellations
      I may not taste

or touch.
Chagrin the name between the banks,
    so many doors down and winded from counting,
      pronouns in acts of substitution,

weirdness in the middle of making promises,
where I am in mind for nothing else
    than to call out,
      to wander ahead with names—

to emerge as the last of the wood-
wind family.
    To call out,
        to utter in

an undertone—
the continents
    in nameable forms, the squid
        that tastes where it touches.

Half Seas Over

Or simply, *drunk*—   Dutch courage in the face of milk and flummery—

our passive margin, our transitional crust, our rift obtusely

known as creation.

     As it lost its concentration, gold was a million things

that *wouldn't* be dragged from ocean:

       crass undertaking

a reason to form—   the sun profounding surface—

       the come-loose asterisks

of starfish bones.

Jardins sous la pluie

You paint precipitation
following thunder: wands of soaked fire, arcs of sea-
revising sun, salt come up to seed in clouds, downfallen cool
and diagonal water.

You paint the garden the garden is: a border blued in
in heavy heads, hydrangeas fed aluminum sulfate,
a border blued up in amended beds, in old
pear peelings and grass.

Moon is to the blueness of panicles as seawater is
to the whiteness of rain. Hours in this feeling
of yours and mine.

Born in the woulds of the given body, waking up
this often there.

Sweet Habit of the Blood

Viburnum's winter fairy globe: in outer robing
it is vivid: a cardinal meal in the drifting bright.

As inner movement understood, radiant caverns
in the out of sight. Up for the habit

of the robust world, the wood boat floating
of a starred green loom.

■

Wherever unsteady

meets with unsteady, there is the lot of physical forms. And guest

and guessed are one to me: whether the sky or whether the lake.

I feel before I want to know: water stays fluid below the frost,

and silver quiets the jargoned heart.

■

Long in the wild of new-ending winter, the exhumed fletcher

could step out
showing his armful of arrows

Is He Decently Put Back Together?

If there is nothing half-assed about the redbud tree, she can be beside it
compositionally, in the form of a spring tableau. See her female

receding to a slight power. Coefficient before a vivid variable,
amplifying, as will the May wind, a purple of the bark-

bearing flowers.
Was it happening to be there, or coming to act

in keeping with one's nature? Who has thought that a soul
is a list of things to be done? Far into the color

of a scene's exaggeration, the lagoon is reading
dreadful words to itself. Looking glass

for the apple in flower,
for that cost of the sky on its surface.

Under the Veil of Wildness

Draw the curtains for candescence.
The antlers were forged by the silversmith.

The sun slips off
auroras, illumines branches of extinction.

Do you call the main body *marker:* a standing
as if instead of? Or else a thing stooped

down upon, and loved? Beneath the tree
a childhood coffer, a penny

and an acorn smell. I call the main body
bramble: verging glow of a crusted switchbox,

on and off until a kind of ending comes.
Looking quietly at a trumpet, a flared bell,

a blackness encompassed by brass, you say *Wait.*
Looking back to the prickers, to the fruit-

picking hand, can you say
Enough? I call the main body

espoused: line of symmetry inside, trench
between two lungs, for the twoness of, the two-

timedness of breathing.
Under the tree, a childhood coffer,

a stashing and a rooting spell.
By oxygen-drawn sheerness into red,

I call the branches to describe themselves.
A body is mainly its branches—

branca claw paw hand—
its tender

and untender branches.

Coming to the Festival of the God of Boundaries

Helios the mute, the keen in Pan's knife.

Some time critical at the bending stream, where he cuts the reeds
at staggered lengths and with the beeswax
begins to bind them.

Beneath the humanly shaped air is an animal's
report of feeling.

Then for the first time saying *or.*

Turning your instrument toward the tree, all the training comes up
as something just below your skin, yet within the business
of the sun. You could be readily alone,
you could be difficult to reach or speak to,

at present included in the subsoil production, where Mercury
scythes the head off Io's warden, Argus, whose every hundred eyes
under the messenger's messenger voice
caves to a slumberous feeling.

In such a beautiful piece
for reeds, it is all ears under the architected
bridal veil, our trinkets working to the surface of earth.

The earth, too,
and moreso tidal, tidal in the congregate
shifts of grazing, tidal in the turn of plow, itself a substance
for the moon's compactments.

Her own voice frightens her. In lowing hearing herself low.
Her father feeds her grass, swats a fly
from her eyelash.

The border completely herbaceous. Quantities of sun
later to be crushed from borage.

To wedge a story inside a story. To cut the trunk radially.
Argus, whose every hundred eyes heard Syrinx running
into sound, Syrinx being chased by everywhere.
Staggered lengths of story.

And does the god have a mind of his own,
Pan in the needles, the unthinkable pine wreath,
a ubiquity darkly seductive of breeze?

Along her various edges, between obvious and audible and covetous,
the rarely dissected textures, fog is condensing into water
on the hardened forewings (shards)
of darkling beetles.

For the reinstatement of a hundred eyes, the covert feathers
snapping into courtship.
Now you: you now.

If affluence
speaks into the mouth, if the very long dead exceed our energy?

In the room adjoining the living room, the offer to play
the nocturne over.

You now: now you—

Makes an Arrangement

Of many stems, the water, lukewarm, the water whose irenic ladder down
to a slant clip in going giving to the stem a greener opening

who gives a   period

and gives   to live in lost continuation

of oneself, sticks caught
in peace of stones, in clouds shaped as a windpipe

at a no more foreign accent

true in the woods
there is in trillium, a wild against the skin

and body the very gesture could be true, body drawn truce
in the pencil-looks of life, from nature

drawn and made of water—drawn of rush, copper, salt—of flowers the earth
why not bestows

what makes me know
in a faucet hue, could silver

warm to be a hue (to bird down, beauty, hide)
time and water rooming

in the ewer base, then you (good
god) is true, and futures on the glass of flower cooler, and past,

a glass (in time comes in), a second-seeded eucalyptus, and drops

on glass, and split-off thoughts, on cooler door,
diminutives of mass—

the molecules, the hand-shaped streaks

Return of the Native to the Widespread Hour

In her yellow caravan, the feather merchant has sold out of wares.

Ambitious only to feel her coat's inner lining, in performing one
normal action backward, she sublimes, she goes beneath
the oldest stone, she greets the interruptive
shake before duration.

Breathe on a harpsichord, and it will sound.
Sink a chunk of salt on your tongue to name the ocean.

The swan's distinctive contour will pinpoint the sky.

So her resources are wanting to reach her:

knowing with a red cloth tied at her neck
where leafage is system to leaves.

Midlander

this region that moves the voice is made of ears

so that a region we are born to

sounds like listening and we seem even older

when we speak this way—like a glow of clay compressed—light

as the hiddenness of the nonapparent

sun being wind along the leaves—among pieces of recognition—

bootprints that said *footsteps* on the day's clean floor—a flox's

violent blue—a word or two more valuable

than those surrounding it or them

because made of what we eventually are (that is the region

a region expanding the accent inward)

glass washes up soft

in fields that are folds of waves for you

without edges to see and weigh it lightly (you)

so that *nearer to the heart* (for me

to say it) is not coming or going but is

the lasting dissolution made particular

as sea glass in the whole blue

distances I

and you inhabit

Thicket Play

I asked the sun to stay outside.

       I called its effort *disentangled*. I put the body
there as marker, held up as if in place of. Or else, a thing stooped
down upon, and snapped.

Pictured then as clasped inside.

Claw paw hand: I made the body as mainly its branches.
       One branch I called the *childhood coffer*.

Inside it were
       the many reasons.

Honey Ants

Northeast of Alice Springs, farther along the Darwin highway,
a place was named Utopia prior to its settlement.

It could be rhythm lies in expectation, and expectation, in memory.
Gum tree, gum tree, no gum tree, gum tree.

Alone again with ochre and a stretch of wall, we know whatever we follow
will sometime come off-center. Sun and hope, dazzling and invisible.
 Our own acts

of touching follow, feeling nothing we cannot alter
by making it consciously so.

Recessive

vertical shadow a rasping of drum
gesso primer covering the grave

motional the wooden panel
under oils that would rest above it

to gray the gold of fallout
squareless in the circle's presence

∎

rabbit skin glue
for keeping dusts together

I have thought the heart and cage
trees through a window raised

to yellow interest by October rain
in relative speeds

∎

to a room's chalk teachings
respiratory hitches for the teacher

shared area of jots
shall we stick together in the black field

widening diamonds of an elevator's grate
lift to disinhabited apartments

∎

runners the color of dying grass
fraud of spy- & cheval glass

the eye was once
the mind for silver leaf

was sylvan
in the sixth sense

where mind was once
the absorbent primer

∎

brilliant in its prefiguration
of moon

though brittle though crabby
and crackable

on canvas more than
it interrupts the shells

∎

it lends them room and seconds
to circle and ascend

the dark water we see through
there and there

when the crest thins the wave
to outstretched liquid

∎

where the sea
shells roll

tilting at the one that stands
for appearance

skull of folded arms and legs
in the cross section

of hillside
prince of all earth

in their formal
setting

a thing
for the mind

to spot
and follow

Sending Owls to Athens

Redundancy redundancy.

       Moon of my collarbone long ago broken.

Moon overlapping my look at the vascular. A dog-eared page says

Neptune green. A fourth type of song

       is performed upon

a cricket's invasion of territory. Broken in

the place of broken. Or nothing would argue my nervous system:

grays in the grays of nephogram, ash tree's flourish

where the library steps.

       Wind in the color—

there is no such thing. No color to color the color.

William James, Henry James

Great gift of purple apples! The distant stars, the far-in sugars
of their skins. With light in certain
shades of the world, *autumn* of limited
use in the world, I could go
for a day
in the word *canteen*.

In the world outside
I have yet to put in. It looks as though the bridges
are standing in aquarelle. You know *propitious*
comes of *going-forward*. Where the horse in mind
unfastens earth, fastens thirst
to a treelike task.

Arethusa

Sequent evening slopes inside, carries the sound of the caller. Distinctly
out of sync, the double rapping of the carpenter frog, mating knock
of the hummock, its earth-swallowed packets, its gists of pollen
in the peat's dark core. Nymph
that the huntress

    dug an escape for—faceless in the weir, an *in* beyond
a glass or dam, escaped *I am* of the mirror
branching. In sequin
switches of light, in wending rash of magnifications.

Thread in. Morning lens
to a bog orchid claw, to its yellow life in the wetland body.

Arrowsic

Oscar Wilde made Narcissus

leafmeal burying the fall in water

to see above the decomposing

first we split a champagne bottle

then swam for the middle

then you noted

language distinction

on the tree

two eyes in which the water loved itself

summer like a coin to pay with

a boy climbed a pine

the graceful shape

of the widening pond

a foreign-

word for the leaf that has stayed

word for the leaf that has not

Eidothea

Some greens are like coins

whose profiles the sea is tossing. If skin like summer is off and on,

if dressed for summer, it runs the grasses.

On the rest of the day, a rareness could land. So long to you

who softened the volume, who called my shadows into blue-

dark hills. Fountains like luck are lucid,

and strange. Or climbing the air

in postures of power.

Sunrise with Sea Monsters

In bulletins of spray to sky, a morning forgets a million yellows.
Stroke of yellow into grainy noun, now a light quarried from yellow.

What is your face on the face of the water? A mirror conceals
it begins in stone. Noun of informing and resuming yellow. Stone steps

inside of mirror, appalling and alighting yellow. Yellow washing onto steps.
Granite that begins in grains. Stars of a monster iris—from yellow

former to former.

Where Hardly Hearth Exists

a turning out to air the contents. Content to say, *I have* or *had,*
   content to have a go.

The hearth bricks round a temperature.

In the kind of sex that is metonym for spirit, glass gets wings
   on rags of sand. Glass,

a sister in feeling, lake-tinted, transparent above all in family.

    For the breastbone's base, a slip in volume, a modest depression
outside the language of anatomy.

    Heart-spoon. Mud-nester, here and after, I give your core
same walls as integer. Elaborate lean-to, where fractions spoon and chime
with sky, in the lowest rank imaginable, in the mining of bones
we know to be mineral.

    Mine the bones. The hearse will float, the horses shed
their shoes for swash. Flowers for a space of flowers.
   To swim a cove at night

at eighteen naked, luminescence slipping from our wrists.

Prior to writing as a form of possession, what lights and shadows
   swept the walls.

Now from the shallows of reverberating furnace:

a wager in the panic-grass of sight: blood-shine of the dahlia

a coming closer thunder, blue soil
of molars, coinage, pollen.

Such being

the bitter angels of our nature, a curse (traditional, Wexford) went

like this:
May the grass
grow on your door and the fox
build his nest on your hearthstone . . .

may the hearthstone
of hell be your best
bed forever.

Gods in every hook

now hang above my hearth. In the eagle's grasp

of Prometheus, in the weirdest grafts & parturitions, in the mulch and dung

of devotion.

      Seeds slippered in core   slight cargo the star in midarchive

of apple

sick, conceivable, wooden.

      Matches & kindling

enough. Switches from a tree for a fire digesting knots and beetles, popping shares of blood—

     no longer a fire

but grass to my knees   green transistor   & sometimes resistor

          (you will know the resistor by a voltage drop across itself)

        no longer a fire

but sometimes an incense: the pocket dictionary I take abroad

embered to one annunciation. Read *coming rain*

onto gathered starlings
     rain into swallowing pinecones:
     open/close open/close

Read articulate glyph of a cold-blooded cricket, of a forewing file and
    scraper.

              Or pick a suffix for heart-

Or pick a prefix for every object you have touched   -   -   -   -

Would it feel more detailed than chronicle, when the mower turns

his face to grass and lays it horizontal as a word?

           One wood lily

spaces the hemlocks.

Name that in sleep goes through the wood and turns around to sleep.

        Forge where I form the feelings,
hearth where the feelings form me. Midden full of artifact, earthful shells
at fruitful bone, utter of intelligible rubble.
Integer you cannot

          count on. *Heart's ease* intensely
growing in the shade. Doubt put off, put on as leaves. Where spoils undress
the weeping beech and go in circles inside it. *Redoubt* the violet,
the pilot light. Sealight put out

put on as leaves.

TWO

I am with him. I am like that old Osiris walking in the night.
Drunk on the cool wine of darkness, I eat the bread of life and
die. I know. I am blessed by mortality.

Sonnet on Fire

Is it the space,

if let inside of, you would remember having lived in
for a particular time? That *thump*

was a bird meeting vertical glass. Something in here
collides with elision. Your eye apprehends what had never

had walls. Mind curls   (night falls)

and afterward, forgets the problem. Much of the blueprint

is rooted to death. Much of the glass

has attributed feeling. In the faultless iris
of a random swamp
some of the cabin

      could disappear. Especially in sundown all its surface
is stunning. Except when it rains,

or grasses move, the walls make no   appreciable sound.

The Bad Infinity

If a line comes to buck, or sag, or trouble the level.

If the granite were polished

it would be darker. If your eye goes to the several

in its utmost temper of peace. Do not think of the wind

as a partial anchoress. Do not think of the water with foliage in it.

The grains are darker when polished, or wet. In your mind especially

the granite can darken.

In the living plant, or animal body.   *In vivo*—

Where the lake plain meets the escarpment.

Fasten on the basal, the matter's angle, a dirt in repose of its own.

I know this taste of your steep decline: the shale and brook inside me.

Comes love, the Devonian geology, sweet fissile

of attention, the old nerves in fresh sheets.

Should the fossil fish, the prehistoric sharks, the human hand, get mud to
  speak.

                                   Swear it.

I went to the ice house and touched the augurs and saws.

I smelled the sawdust of storage. Smelled the blocks grappled from pond.

And all the while—

skaters skating as the ice was thick.

Sugary, so sugary to the eye the marble under acid rain.

Limestone, the open dossier.

       Sea lily stems. Sutures in the arch-
angel Michael.

   And the fruit of righteousness is sown
    in peace of them that make peace

      At the arcing shoot, at the winter chest. I quarried
Euclid bluestone. I queried the careful pickax.

      There to there the clouds would offer. Bags with holes
that facts shot through.

Both thumbs on a stone in childhood ambivalence.

Sandbars to rest the fringes of swimming.

Baroque

The substance could come out of the adventure, like a mussel shell
could be

elaborate as cabbages, or the privacy
that keeps its analogue

on the blue bridge waiting.

Miscellany

The linen warp, the woolen weft. The billion, the blazon, the blimey, the broth. The hash, the pewter, the goulash, the brass. *Slink:* the vertebrae in spades. The mixed thing, the steel, the scramble. The coal, the caul, the caller. The muller, the mortar, the mollification. The graphic mistaking of *taste* for *haste.* The profiteer, the privateer, the vulture skull. The paradoxical passage. The lead veins in the window, the wing veins in the Morpho. The high road negotiated by knuckles. The phanopoeia, the melopoeia, the logopoeia. The veil the voile the fog the tulle. The sempiternal overstating. The wincey, the niche-switched, the weirdly converged. The mammal bones, the checkerblooms. Your pocket knife, my abalone. The owl's sclerotic ring.

Baroque

I have turned the kettle on to forgetting.

This can't get away from itself to be a thought. It is not
a whistler, it will not whistle when
it's ready.

A General Discrimination of Synonyms

turn over the word *converse* to watch the idea lifting inside it
like a width of air belted with water, or see in the visible
substance of hourglass a taper of sand focusing
one altitude on another. This is

to turn in the passage of said-to-mean, to remove to
the movement of labyrinth, systems auditory and vestibular,
to the nervous, heavy-scented maze, its boxwood hedges
secluding clouds (a maze being roughly

coterminous with labyrinth, except that it does have
dead ends). To feel in your mind the strange opposition
of thesaurus to dictionary, you must fill in
the trace fossil, the burrow where

an animal went,
turn to this one conclusion: that no synonymy was ever
on the level, synonymy being most itself when stopping weirdly
shy of itself, in the branching, loose-ends

work of words, in the crusted rope that moors the boat
whose stern paint the salt has unscripted
out on the long and most
contingent ocean

where the *salubrity* of the water is being determined,
where a squid is blacking in the margins, where dolphins arc
and go below, where all our options are not the same—
transparency—semitransparency—

opacity—and all our options
are not the same—*healthfulness, wholesomeness,
nutritiousness, salubrity—soundness, aptness,
rightness, goodness.*

Baroque

Under whose ascending rungs
the interior is gutted

                    and started again.

                Modern. Sustainable. Minimal.

Lady of the smokebush,
gray in the act of mauve.

Don't move.

There is a worse thing,
I wager, than being seen.

Antonyms & Intermediaries

Desire is to indifference as indifference, to aversion.

Who is moved to encounter is in the beginning
at home in all shapes before the end. Shine a distance
on this working sail: in the beginning was the making
of ships, and the ships were made
by the grace of trees.

Off-broken earth, moon of long measures, appear to us
to help us appear.

Baroque

Little Dipper—
Extravagant utensil.

First Inspirations of the Nitrous Oxide, Pneumatic Institute, 1799

the purpose is not to explain the significance of words
they being apparently obscured by the clouds
in endless succession, rolling darkly down the stream
in which were many luminous points similar

they being apparently obscured by the clouds
often experienced on rising suddenly
in which were many luminous points similar
and stretching out the arms

often experienced on rising suddenly
after sitting long in one position
and stretching out the arms
incapable of speaking

after sitting long in one position
consciousness of where I was
incapable of speaking
who was near me

consciousness of where I was
my whole frame
who was near me
I thought I panted violently

my whole frame
I felt a singing in my ears
I thought I panted violently
as if their velocity had been suddenly accelerated

I felt a singing in my ears
the bursting of a barrier
as if their velocity had been suddenly accelerated
the actions of inspiring and expiring

the bursting of a barrier
in which were many luminous points similar
the actions of inspiring and expiring
they being apparently obscured by the clouds

Baroque

Thatchwork. Threnody. Theogeny. The earth in all its ill-

imagined parts

        did issue does issue will issue

           Sleeping out of doors in the out-of-doors

    ■   ■   ■

the rest is made of what

Second Inspirations of the Nitrous Oxide

I.

In the spring of 1799, at age twenty, following his self-administration
of nitrous oxide, Roget wrote in his report to the Pneumatic Institution,

*I cannot remember that I experienced the least pleasure
from any of these sensations. . . . And as it is above two months
since I made the experiment, many of the minuter circumstances
have probably escaped me.*

Humphry Davy, a year older than Roget,
and the Institute's superintendent,
found that inhalations effected desirable
changes in his poetry. Breathing nitrous oxide
while walking the hills at Clifton,
near Bristol, he composed lines like these:

*Yet are my eyes with sparkling luster fill'd;
Yet is my mouth replete with murmuring sound;
Yet are my limbs with inward transports filled;
And clad with newborn mightiness around.*

[contemporaries Coleridge and Southey are meanwhile envisioning
the banks of the Susquehanna as the site of their pantisocracy.]

II.

In our childhood, my brother and I had teeth pulled
under laughing gas. As we came back to thinking
in a shared recovery room, we roared at everything that moved,
or spoke—or did an absurd impersonation of doing both.

III.

To arrive at the core of "green" in my thesaurus
I go through the thinking of "greenness"—

virescence, verdancy, verdure—through the feeling of green places—
sward, park, greenbelt, turf—through the music of its pigments—*celadonite,*
chlorophyll, viridian—

through ephemera of green things—*chrysoprase, spinach, putting green*—
through green figures

of speech—*greenroom, greenhorn, green thumb*—
to compounds escaping
parts of speech—*Nile-green, leek-green, sea-green*—
lime-green—dull-green—leaf-green.

IV.

The last of Roget's major labors, begun in 1849 in his seventieth year,
and published in 1852 as *The Thesaurus of English Words and Phrases,*
had few detractors. One of these, E. P. Whipple, said this
of the work in the *North American Review:*

Seriously, we consider this book as one of the best
of a numerous class, whose aim is to secure the results without
imposing the tasks of labor, to arrive at ends by a dexterous
dodging of means, to accelerate the tongue
without accelerating the faculties.

It is an outside remedy for an inward defect. In our opinion, the work mistakes
the whole process by which living thought makes its way into living words . . .

In the mind of Whipple, Roget's *Thesaurus* made a dangerous move
to separate words from feelings, *to shrivel up language*
into a mummy of thought.

V.

Using his knowledge of biological classification, Roget had,
one must admit, done something backward, plotting every word
of the thesaurus, by outline and tabular organization,
into six major classes
of ideas:

    I. Abstract Relations
   II. Space
  III. Matter
  IV. Intellect
   V. Volition
  VI. Sentient and Moral Powers

                            To get *to* the words,
he forked ideas into sections and heads, so that under
class IV—"Intellect"—one would have found under section II,
Precursory Conditions and Operations,
the following "heads":

  Curiosity
  Incuriosity
  Discrimination
  Indiscrimination

VI.

Having left the "irregular" Institute behind,
Roget was, a few years later, wearing green glasses against the glare
in trips beyond Geneva

        to see the glaciers.

THREE

I am a field enduring, growing wheat one year, barley the next, tangled flowering papyrus, a hill of sand. I am everafter, changing, while the eye of the watcher shines and takes me in.

Disheveled Holiness

In the great while under
the monkey puzzle tree, the mockingbird learns
to rusted gate. He will not go so far. He will not find the words.

But will his throat, not rust, but taking its time to sound,
leave, in tracks of rain, a color of rust inside you, or make, as if
he knew, the air a means of import?

From the chanting bird, from the word *stronger*—
from the funny tree, the evergreen.
            Living fossil,

what has come over you?

    It would puzzle a monkey to climb that. The spiky
points, the injury. *Not far from the invention of fire, we must rank
the invention of doubt.*

       Who is here, is here. To abide. To be kind.

To be sound in skeptic combat with the stronger
sound of waves—the practiced sound of waves—the practical

       thinking there.

Medieval Physics

Thousands of rulers up
and the wings are a copied motility

and a cabin is for breathing above the earth
and for walking in on elsewhere.

Why not a horse
now that the fields are visible?

The sun is always
circling the story. Like how

you showed me
how the hummingbirds feed:

saying *This is a moat*
                     and pointing

A Boredom of Spirit

leading to accident. A child among knives, mallets, and punches.
The awl slips in his eye.

Morning that comes like an altered ear, according to birds,
according to coughs.

World that goes on beyond the evident. Vibrant rocks
at the edge of the brook. Radishes revolving in water. The butterfly duskiest
nearest the body
to keep the ovaries warm.

Louis Braille. This is how the stars move. This is how to set the table.
This is the smell of a heating oven. Listen and remember.

Slant rains all day, and thunder. At organ practice, crosswinds audible
through glass. Paris coming apart in bells.

How then?

Not reading *rive* on pins.
Not soldiers nightwriting in the dark.

The milk wagons wake him from a dream, a rope gang long enough
to wander Paris.

Louis Braille. Braille. The world goes on.
Six dots to a cell, and passages of it
raised above surface.

Gothic Tropical

Is the oculus I omitted from the higher
story, the detailed forgetting of orbital bones.

Pinned thing, a common Pierrot,
heir to the room's declining momentum.

Close to finest ossicle,
The storm is being bargained down.

Window, you feel the last of it:
elucidation's dropping value, dark, the after-

thought of switch,
the fan in a flower of paddles.

Film in Place of a Legal Document

Where the green pump calls for wonderful arms
to bring up water in iron gulps

pan left: to distant fluctuations, to hooves freaking
insects out of grass.

The soundtrack said: *You think your thirst
arcs from the waterspout when in fact
it arcs from the ground.*

Sinister, like a ventriloquist draining a glass of water
while making
a whole statuary sing.

To the left of the linden in June, to the left of the graveyard's
human quiet

a neighbor worked a pneumatic hammer.

It was left to the ocean to matchstick the hull,
left to the darkroom to develop the trees.

Japonisme

I am not choosing
between function and ornament.

Were there
a parasol. Were it ribbed to shed

a painful brightness from the eyes.
Could it spread its flowers at the shining

waves, you could open it now,
if you cared to.

Against the Throne and Monarchy of God

Moon to light the spaces of the glossary. Birdless oak
of folded wings, shadows clotting the moon-green crown.

Meal of a moth, out for the moon.
Meal of a fish and a thorn apple's nectar.

Meal of milk.
Piecemeal.

Moon to light the loophole in mammalian
laws of gravity. Not hand or wing

in the oak. Not *home:*
home in.

Acousmatic

Not a concept, much less a faith—
not quiet

but coming forward from the dust, a white mare
partially bone, primarily fast in the higher field.

And was the sound of snow dissolving,
glass being blown from lips of beginners?

Where by *love* I mean a failing, copious
and opaque, heart without a practical power

most feeling the gives of undone.
Fountain and basin, the water penned in,

the tension to ring where the water
turns down, where the beads

are cracking our sun's white codex
in the courtyard foreign beyond

the window, plurally into something else.
When I live on the look of muteness, where I lived

on the look of happiness,
rose that was quanta—

I ask after cost—after gouge of grass
and sky, after cause

that hides its cause
in unsustainable shapes of pain,

in tempos habituating grass,

redbud trees in arriving and splitting—

accost, accost, come closer to my ribs.
Not only the understanding

has a language, be it wind
in rings of meanest direction,

or deepest remove when bluest in surface.
By *memory* I mean a skin: a cover

for the underworlds
that we might try to breathe,

or hear in wind a single,
soothing thing,

or hear of wind a kindred displacement—
in our skins to the added

subtractions we live in, sun over sand, the coppered hem-
wetness, sun in tons of bells, in apples cut open

to disappear—yes, now I am listening
to your fallible sounds

pity for the you that is stranded,
pity for the you that is only

a voice, where now I am hearing
a mechanical click

to see I had no beautiful shelter
the motioning colors of the trees, the edgewise

pit before beginning
to take up

listening as something harder, to take up
walking as something longer

attach me, walking, attach me

The Orator's Maximal Likelihood

On the strength of its first thread, a spider commits
design, commits its body's lengths to measurements of silk.

There is a hard work you ate in honey.
There is a hard work in parts of speech. In turning your heart
to a pulpit, you captured a sample of persuasion: gray, the passenger
pigeons, the migrateurs, gray the epigraphical palettes, the small,
uncertain laughter at the cages of doves.

Where is now the feeling of the law, human in
the dullest outline? The errand is all about you: a demon sings,
the song is yours, a fog catcher catches condensation.

In the law of truce and probability.
In the law of the horse coming down from the hill. A left-out word like
gossamer. A word left out
like grace.

Interior shades suggesting evening: dark pink like an anatomical page,
dark pink
like an ivory lampshade.

A word, then, for who will conquer it?

To the hands suggesting prayer, cream white corymbs
of the rowan in flower. Law of soft, and softer work.
Law of excavation. Faintest in
its truest outline, law of the coming thing.

The Beauty of Where We Have Been Living

This takes hold of soil and here. In the same way sun
flowers the sea, in the same way seeds

lie in the light. A buoy bell rocks
above a farm's long furrows. Granite is over

and under the living. Through a loom
leaned on a sunlit wall, warp-ends weighted

down with clay, a Monarch works
as floating through, as saying to, as otherwise.

Could I pass all words through the end of seeing,
new would rise to speak of working.

New moon, full stop, black-apple phase.
Will grow a crescent presence over days, will give

(by light) your name to snow
and blossom.

Anatomy of Listening

Soft bouncing of the paper lights. A pair of shutters
unhooked from the inside.

I cut you a reed, I pass you a pipe.   I wish you a waterway unnatural.

We have talked over time on the movement of swans:
canal a form of irrigation

                     canal a form of transportation. In this sense
we are certain companions: in my ears

we are breaking bread.

Sighting

There are hours when a creek

                crops brightest from rocks. The exchange of gifts

known as *nothing is missing.*

      There's a marsh most its own

without the sun

   in a *then*

        like a lord of appearance. There's a contour that grazes

merely on rain—

      dead bone of antlers lowered in dark—

a doubting that blurs the demarcation,

        & the raising, hazeled in headlights.

If It Be Not Now

Brief sparrow, rye-light, what is your stance? The air
in memoriam stings. The sun has all it needs.

At the liquid side of firs, on the snowy wind,
is there its spring, in the open cold, a renaissance,

a resin coming in to lung
to stick awhile in rocky apses?

Off course, such a long way in, what Providence
in the body's corpus, in the revolutionary second hand?

Voice from the flanks of avalanche. And another under
the slit of waves.

Killer your blue, an optic banner cloudless sky—
the stand the wait

on the wordless slope
that gives no sign of being burial.

This Daniel & lion—those carnelian steppes in cameo—
that tomorrow you put my hands out for.

I have a splinter.
I have it well. That love might call me more than fear, I feel,

I think, the preferential scatterings. Blue photons
like a camera in a river. Air for the ribbon

to fall through. Fire to light
survival's finish.

Ovation

It is possibly warmer than Hades in here.

Sewn to slats of whalebone,
a rainbow brightening air, what remains of the Carolina Parakeet—
saffron, lemon, viridian—a wrist snaps open to fan.

Small miracles go out in summary. At last the opera curtain rises,
and most of the house, after clearing its throats, goes still.

                  The *tin man* gene is said to make a fly's heart.
Seeing that it will eat the dead, evolution (not to say *beautifully*)
bares the vulture's head. The tenor exhales
a high C forte.

When the lyre was fished from the violent river, the stars took
wing around it. Near Draco and Cygnus, we can choose which bird
we imagine falling.
                 Aquila cadens, Vultur cadens

To make the heart fly, the barn owl opens
its face in trees.

Or passes the mallows in other names—

delicate owl   *straw owl*   *rat owl*   *death owl*

Morse Gives Up Portraiture

To swing from a broken current. Knob, the brass apple,
for this side of rooms. Oak tree thick in the door.

Atlantic, the holding of breath. Airtight
in gutta-percha gum, the telegram

comes out of the water. The nap is stopped
from going deeper. A rowboat, a fin,

a coming feeling.
Bright thread in dry fingers.

Absence tapping its home and twilight.
No one touching the piano.

Intrinsic

Unmistakable shape upon the eye, the kite is far above me, a black tail
deeply forked. Inside what follows, within the feeling of the river,

the kite might go from flesh to fruit, from frog, from nestling,
to fig, or pawpaw.

Follow a bird aboard its shadow, by the carry of its cry, into the angle
of its kill. *Only something that has no history can be defined.*

Kee-kle-klee. Deeply forked, the black tail. Sharp shape upon the eye,
and closer still, blue-black with, in growing light, the underworldly

reign of iridescence.
When I shake with purpose, I have no idea. Spring could be

a set of days. Or a strand of being
the wind knows how to play.

This could be immature forever, the rufous bloom of its upper breast
not to fade how things fade in the sea.

Why I shake with purpose, I have no idea.
Why I keep such keys.

Continuous coming through the doors, sounds for the hallway's
unlit feeling.

Intimations

Museum darkness has its natural history. Back in the planetarium,
I am pretending closer to the exotic classes, the blue stragglers
in much higher temperatures.

The audience extends from there. A silhouette crop,
washed in what looks like television.

I came through my birth a little bit ragged. My feeling comes spacey
or faintly populous. I can't say *souls* and know what I'm saying. Still,
Tiffany glass has fumes inside it: every Sunday's daylight
knows this. *Ummm*

goes the Venetian piva. I look to the doge enfolding the balcony.
The lutes like halves of pears have stopped.

That was no game of hangman.

Now what will he put in the sky?

A book of all moons. The shadows in Galileo's head.

The body is always being educated.
Theater is like this. The planetarium is like this.

The whale is not hurt or in any way ruined.
The whale is a great lightness.

Constable of the Sweet Oblong

In the unrehearsed glimpse of the brown bottle is the habit of sun to spot
    everything.

You have caught the orange mood

flouting closer earlier.

                Where the gardener calls his raised bed

Moon garden   —

        Where the hyssop's square stem, the drawn-from

career of cloud, a light whipped over in aspect of wall   —

bare barrier

(call name, wait for hand)

                    In the start of autumn, hips in the roses.

In the door made foreign by a pattern of grain. In the divers forms

of calling attendance.

Work

Nothing to gossip over: white oak shadows, a current
manifolding gold. As was the news

from nowhere: the vegetable dye, the longerwhile
of replication, to weave of the river, *Evenlode.*

There is no place the mourning cloak lifts up.
There is nowhere the question mark doesn't light down.

The tent is on fire
with all you have owned: the known

to be useful, the believed to be beautiful.
The oak lobes are.

The river is. The earth will have us.
Repeat and repeat.

Salon/Saloon

Outside the sediment in the broadest sense. Inside we make

in talk and smoke

a fire to drink and gaze inside of.

When you reach for the glass—

                wake like the waterbirds make in fall

                maple-maple on the water

                love like a pond on the heart of my brain

                      —shall I move in it

unusually tailored, in my only suit dyed to a wood duck's green?

Can we watch us walk in the drinking mirror

                [or bite or fly or make a warning call]

in the oval measure of the fiery

                place (no pond) (no grass), the oiled wood booths

                (no grass) (no edge)

—can we watch us go for a glass of beer—you in my vest

as I reach for your glass—*shank crown*   *arm fluke*—the anchor at

the end of glass?

Strokes

the comb gave out a different honey
when the farmer went under
the fallow acre
and they told his bees with a black cloth flag

1849—a camp chicken's gizzard made gold disclosures
it had been eating gold
somewhere where
sun changed water to water

{gain-}

what survives of a once-common prefix
no longer active in compounds—

{say}

the load of hay approaching
is wished upon

the wish is to be fulfilled
when the bale is broken open

Building Box (Atlantic)

Though the moon is no saw it shows a taste for wood
it ranges through wood as deep as blood, blood
still good for building astonishment.

Sail that goes
behind a crop of coast. How crops and enlargements
get in to the useful. Squirm of sail

on the rough-to-touch. *Come back*
it goes
come back.

Posthumous

It is late when the rummage gets underway. The air smells more
of earth than decks. Dockhands brag
to pretty bonnets, cormorants spear at wavy profits.

Now for a password

to work at all. For "walnut" to open
a single star.

I'm done with the worst of cursed and cursing.

When the wind stands me up
so I do not fall, I'll forget which psalm
works against which sin.

Oratorium

Lap the evening water where it blackens. Cat where I cannot see
habit the light in cells. Morning would have a river in its mouth.

Oil of the flower's every step. Never a word, neither a star—
but blue to the end of remembering.

Summer Reading

Up in the middle of the yard
is a fishing net being mended in good light. So that even

      the atheist's novel was a place to choose to live.
Bound together for motion in sunshine, the pages felt more
than a few lives long. Flowers orange

and joyful-yellow, but stuck in dusts
of human traffic, the jewelweed & touch-me-nots

      could release
their contents
at the slightest brush. *It is better—it shall be better with me*

because I have known you.
Can I hope to say it

      in any case? To blossom is thoughtless—
so we barely leave room
for each other to blossom.

Summer: the wild carrot umbel went to seed.
Summer: the wild carrot umbel could recite

      the bird nest's negative space. I am not afraid
of the concave shape. These were our common names—
the names for which

we had something in common.

Notes

I borrow my book title from a line in Wallace Stevens's poem "Repetitions of a Young Captain."

"Greeting Osiris" excerpts, used as epigraphs for section markers 1, 2, and 3, come from Normandi Ellis's translation of the Egyptian Book of the Dead: *Awakening Osiris* © 1988 used with permission of Phanes Press, an imprint of Red Wheel/ Weiser, LLC <redwheelweiser.com>.

SALT MARSH, THICK WITH BEHAVIORS

The Comma landing in and flying out of the sentence "A woman should behave herself naturally" is a species of butterfly and also a punctuation mark that alters, ever so slightly, some lines borrowed from *The Philadelphia Story:*

George Kittredge:	But a man expects his wife to . . .
Tracy Lord:	Behave herself. Naturally.
C. K. Dexter Haven:	To behave herself naturally.
	[George gives him a look]
C. K. Dexter Haven:	Sorry.

JARDINS SOUS LA PLUIE

After one of the 1967 Ceri Richards paintings by this title.

SWEET HABIT OF THE BLOOD

I borrowed this phrase from George Eliot.

COMING TO THE FESTIVAL OF THE GOD OF BOUNDARIES

Termine, sive lapis sive es defossus in agro
stipes, ab antiquis tu quoque numen habes.

Terminus, whether you are a stone or a stump buried in the field, from ancient days you too have been possessed of numen. (OVID, *Fasti,* Book 2)

Thanks to Juliana Froggatt and Richard Gridley for help with this translation.

RECESSIVE

This poem is an attempted conversation with the "Janicon" series of artist Paul Feiler.

SUNRISE WITH SEA MONSTERS

After the J. M. W. Turner painting.

THE BAD INFINITY

Written after a geological walking tour of the Lakeview Cemetery in Cleveland, Ohio.

MISCELLANY

Peter Mark Roget kept a classification notebook when he was only eight years old. One of the section headings was "Different Things" (a miscellany). This poem works with synonyms for the word *miscellany,* and with miscellaneous items from my own notebooks.

A GENERAL DISCRIMINATION OF SYNONYMS

. . . far less do I venture to thrid [*sic*] the mazes of the vast labyrinth into which I should be led by any attempt at a general discrimination of synonyms. The difficulties I have had to contend with have already been sufficiently great, without this addition to my labours. (PETER MARK ROGET)

ANTONYMS & INTERMEDIARIES

In many cases, two ideas which are completely opposed to each other, admit of an intermediate or neutral area, equidistant from both; all these being expressible by corresponding definite terms. (PETER MARK ROGET)

FIRST INSPIRATIONS OF THE NITROUS OXIDE

All the language in this pantoum is Roget's, taken verbatim from two sources: from a report he made to the Pneumatic Institute following his self-administration of the gas and (in smaller portions) from his introduction to his *Thesaurus*.

SECOND INSPIRATIONS OF THE NITROUS OXIDE

My information about Roget comes from D. L. Emblem's biography, *Peter Mark Roget: The Word and the Man* (New York: Thomas E. Crowell, 1970). This poem is for Jane Grogan, who, at age ten, made this sentence in response to grammar homework: *The musician has many guitars, but tonight he strummed his green guitar.*

DISHEVELED HOLINESS

Borrows from Whitman's "Out of the Cradle Endlessly Rocking" and directly quotes T. E. Huxley (aka "Darwin's Bulldog"). In his book *Coleridge's Metaphors of Being* (Princeton University Press, 1979), Edward Kessler used the phrase "disheveled holiness" to describe Coleridge's sense of divinity.

AGAINST THE THRONE AND MONARCHY OF GOD

Title taken from line 42 of Milton's *Paradise Lost* (Book 1, "The Argument").

ACOUSMATIC

This poem is for Mark and Elizabeth.

THE ORATOR'S MAXIMAL LIKELIHOOD

In statistics, "maximal likelihood" is a method used to fit a mathematical model to data. Estimating maximal likelihood helps to tune the "free parameters" of the model to real-world data.

THE BEAUTY OF WHERE WE HAVE BEEN LIVING

This poem is for my goddaughter, Lucy (May 25, 1994–July 21, 2006). The title is drawn from Robert Duncan's "Salvages: An Evening Piece": *The tide of our purpose has gone back into itself, into its own counsels. And it is the beauty of where we have been living that is the poetry of the hour.*

Only something that has no history can be defined is taken from Nietzsche.

Homage to William Morris, author of the utopian socialist novel *News from Nowhere;* designer of the Evenlode textile pattern; and all-around good thinker: "Have nothing in your house that you do not know to be useful, or believe to be beautiful."

The atheist is George Eliot. The novel (from which I quote) is *Daniel Deronda.*

Acknowledgments

I am very grateful to the journals that first published these poems, some in slightly different forms and by slightly different titles:

Aufgabe:	Intimations
	Strokes
Cerise Press:	Jardins sous la pluie
	Sweet Habit of the Blood
Chicago Review:	A Boredom of Spirit
	Building Box (Atlantic)
	Where Hardly Hearth Exists
Crazyhorse:	Anatomy of Listening
	Sunrise with Sea Monsters
Denver Quarterly:	If It Be Not Now
Fourteen Hills:	Arethusa
	Morse Gives Up Portraiture
Gray Tape:	Gothic Tropical
Greatcoat:	Eidothea
	Oratorium
	Recessive
Gulf Coast:	Disheveled Holiness
Harp & Altar:	Film in Place of a Legal Document
	Sending Owls to Athens
	Thicket Play
jubilat:	Acousmatic

Kenyon Review Online:	The Beauty of Where We Have Been Living
	Medieval Physics
Mudlark:	Honey Ants
	Is He Decently Put Back Together?
	The Orator's Maximal Likelihood
	Ovation
	Return of the Native to the Widespread Hour
NEO:	Against the Throne and Monarchy of God
	Salt Marsh, Thick with Behaviors
	Table of Consanguinity (The Cousin Chart)
	Work
New American Writing:	The Bad Infinity
	Salon/Saloon
Pool:	Intrinsic
Slope:	Coefficient
	Half Seas Over
	Makes an Arrangement
	Midlander
	Miscellany
	Posthumous
	Sonnet on Fire
	Summer Reading
The Tusculum Review:	Arrowsic
	Coming to the Festival of the God of Boundaries
	Constable of the Sweet Oblong
	Diminution of the Clear Thing

"Under the Veil of Wildness" is reprinted in Camille T. Dungy et al., eds., *From the Fishouse: An Anthology of Poems That Sing, Rhyme, Resound, Syncopate, Alliterate, and Just Plain Sound Great* (New York: Persea Books, 2009).

I want to thank my family, friends, students, and teachers. For sending me all the way from China a stamp of "gladness" ("Ru Yi"—or, "the heart's content") with complementary bright red ink, I want to give very special thanks to Qun. Thank you for sharing this stamp—and brightening its way—so generously. Thanks also to Chris Flint, whose careful translation of passages from "The Spiritual Canticle" of St. John, though they do not ultimately appear in the book, were not for naught!

NEW CALIFORNIA POETRY

edited by	Robert Hass
	Calvin Bedient
	Brenda Hillman
	Forrest Gander

For, by Carol Snow
Enola Gay, by Mark Levine
Selected Poems, by Fanny Howe
Sleeping with the Dictionary, by Harryette Mullen
Commons, by Myung Mi Kim
The Guns and Flags Project, by Geoffrey G. O'Brien
Gone, by Fanny Howe
Why/Why Not, by Martha Ronk
A Carnage in the Lovetrees, by Richard Greenfield
The Seventy Prepositions, by Carol Snow
Not Even Then, by Brian Blanchfield
Facts for Visitors, by Srikanth Reddy
Weather Eye Open, by Sarah Gridley
Subject, by Laura Mullen
This Connection of Everyone with Lungs, by Juliana Spahr
The Totality for Kids, by Joshua Clover
The Wilds, by Mark Levine
I Love Artists, by Mei-mei Berssenbrugge
Harm., by Steve Willard
Green and Gray, by Geoffrey G. O'Brien
The Age of Huts (compleat), by Ron Silliman
Selected Poems, 1974–2006: it's go in horizontal, by Leslie Scalapino
rimertown/an atlas, by Laura Walker
Ours, by Cole Swensen
Virgil and the Mountain Cat: Poems, by David Lau

Designer *Claudia Smelser*   Text and Display *Garamond Premier Pro*
Compositor *BookMatters, Berkeley*   Printer *Maple-Vail Book Manufacturing Group*

■